The Struggles
of a Man

Manhood

Demoine Kinney

Manhood

The Struggles of a Man

By: Demoine Kinney

Pure Thoughts Publishing, LLC

Copyright

All Scripture quotation, unless otherwise indicated, are taken from the Holy Bible, New International Version®. NIV®. Copyright © 1973, 1978, 1984 by International Bible Society. Used by permission of

Zondervan Publishing House. Buss, D. M. (1995)
"The Evolution of Desire"; Strategies of Human
Mating, Basic Books.

ISBN- 13 978-1-943409-08-2

Library of Congress Control Number: 2015959983

Printed in the United States of America.

Dedication

This book is dedicated to all the men that are struggling with figuring out who they are and why it is important to stay connected to the source of all things, which is God. I pray that this is an encouraging tool that can be used by men both young and old. I am sharing a few of my personal struggles so that you will see how God has worked with me and allowed me to see Him in all the situations in my life. Some of you may have gone through the same experiences or similar situations.

Table of Contents

Introduction

This portion of the book is dedicated to all of the hardworking men that are willing to go above and beyond, for not only themselves, but for their families and communities.

Being a man can be a hard task if one is not equipped with all the necessary tools to be called a man. Many young boys look at men they want to be like, but really don't know what it takes to become like that man that they are seeing. For instance, a lot of young men watch wrestling and boxing and think it is just about rolling around on the ground or throwing a punch, when there is a lot more to it than that. The truth is that it takes a lot of time and learning in order to become effective at any sport. You need to learn the basics first, and then you move on to other fundamental principles, such as strength training, endurance, and stamina.

These three things can take you a long way if used at the right times and in the right environments. Many young boys think that it is necessary to be hard and not show any emotion at all, but the reality is that that is not human. NEWS FLASH, MEN, YOU'RE NOT AN ANIMAL! In their lifetime, every human being has or will experience something that makes them feel an unexplainable emotion toward something or someone. There is nothing wrong with expressing how you feel about someone or something that is of importance to you. The problem nowadays is that people show emotion toward things that do not even matter, so they become confused with the things that actually matter to them. Men are especially guilty of this, because at times we allow ourselves to be pulled into situations that are not meant for us. For instance, say a woman comes up to a man and tells him a sad story about how bad her life is and how she was raised in a broken home. Instantly, the man will feel moved to try to help fix the issue, when in actuality, he was raised in a broken home himself and has the same emotional issues as the young lady, but he just deals with it differently.

The man may become confused, because he is trying to help someone with an issue that he is dealing with himself. Instead of both of them seeking counseling, they'll try to help each other, which may start something called a relationship. Without realizing how badly this may turn out, they begin on a journey that they think is going to be great, when in actuality, it cannot become great, because the issues haven't been addressed. Men, we cannot save anyone from a past that we weren't a part of. Women want a man to make them feel secure, but you cannot do that if you aren't secure within yourself. Many men have issues that they have kept on the inside for years that need to be dealt with, like child molestation, for example. As young boys, we are taught to be strong and not to cry about the things we are going through, because girls do that. I'm here to tell you that emotional feelings are natural and crying is natural. If you weren't meant to cry, you wouldn't have tear ducts in your eyes.

A lot of people believe that molestation only happens to females, but I'm here to tell you that is not true. Many boys are exposed to things like pornography at a very young age. Personally, I remember seeing family members watching pornography on television and turning it off when other adults walked in the house. I also remember seeing street hustle men sell pornography to children at the young age of 12 and 13. Exposure to things like pornography opens up doors for the enemy, and he will walk right in and take over an innocent child. I used to ask myself the question "Why is it that only females are always recognized as rape victims, when men get raped too? It isn't always a man raping a woman in this world; women rape men too." Things can seem so innocent when you are a child, but when you get older, you realize what really happened.

Kids often play a game called House, and they have mommas, daddies, and children. Everything is set up just like a real family, but then comes the part when the mommas and daddies go into their bedroom, and things start to happen with the children. Children start to get curious and wonder what adults do, so they use their imaginations, as kids do. They start kissing each other and touching each other in places that kids shouldn't. That fast, things can go from an innocent little game to rocky territory. Most young boys do not know not to touch little girls, unless they are taught by their parents, but most parents do not suspect that their child would be doing things like that. When a man experiences things like this at a young age, doors of whoredom and homosexuality could open up.

When I was a child, there was a young boy who didn't like girls, and he always wanted to lay down with the little boys. He used to touch the younger kids, and they would cry to the day care provider, but she didn't think the boy was really touching them in that way - until the day when he pulled a little boy's clothes down and tried to have sex with him. After that incident, they didn't allow the boy to be around the younger kids, and eventually he was taken out of the day care. I am a witness to what happens after situations like this, because now the young boy is dressing like a woman and dates men, while the child who was molested by the older boy struggles with his manhood so much that he feel like he has to overcompensate. He has been in and out of jail and has never talked about this situation from his childhood.

The problem with a lot of men is that we do not talk about situations that have caused us pain and hurt, because we feel like no one will understand. The truth is that there are people who understand your pain, because someone out there has gone through something similar to you. It is not considered being soft to ask for help, the situation could cause you more pain in the future. Many men have things that have hurt them in the past that they will take to their graves, but there is no need for that. Get help now, so you can move on and have an enjoyable life without stressing over a situation from your childhood.

"Whatever we plant in our subconscious mind and nourish with repetition and emotion will one day become a reality."

Earl Nightingale

When His Joy Falls

Great men are they who see that the spiritual is stronger than any material force, that thoughts rule the world.

- Ralph Waldo Emerson

Chapter 1

A scenario I would like to mention that a lot of men do not talk about is molestation by a family member or family friend. Jaden is 10 years old, and he is standing in his living room alone, trying to figure out how to hook up the PlayStation. He hears footsteps, so he drops the cords and sits on the couch. He feels someone getting closer, and the person proceeds to walk into the room. "What you doing, lil' man?" the adult says. "Nothing, just trying to play the game. My dad usually hooks it up for me, but he's at work," Jaden says. "I can hook it up for you, but what are you going to do for me?" the adult says. "You can play with me if you want,"

Jaden says. "That sounds good to me, but why don't you play with me," the adult says.

Just that fast, something could happen, and an innocent 10-year-old child could be in a very compromising position with this adult, who is a family friend. Many young men go through this and are scared to tell someone, because they may have been threatened by the adult or may just be embarrassed about what happened. A lot of the men who go through this grow up to become very abusive, very promiscuous, and very violent, or even start to show signs of homosexual behavior. Parents have to be mindful and aware of what is going on in their homes, and it is a must that kids sit down and talk with their parents. Many children feel like they can't talk to their parents because their parents act as if they were perfect when they were children.

It is 'time out' for prideful attitudes when your children are trying to talk to you and just want to feel like what they are saying really matters to you. If you don't give children the attention they need and deserve, they will go find it in other places, and these things can be prevented. I know some may say that you can't control the actions of others, but don't be that one parent who is caught by surprise when something is going on and doesn't find out until it is too late. Parents, I would like to make you aware of something - just because you may have adult friends doesn't mean they are going to be nice, kind, or respectful to your children.

If your children tell you something about a friend of yours, do not automatically assume the child is lying just because you have been friends with the accused person for any period of time. You may think you know your friends very well, but there may be a few things your friend has been hiding because they are embarrassed about the demons they struggle with. I believe children can see things that adults sometimes either can't see, or may be overlooking based on their desire to feel like they have friends. Oftentimes, children aren't trying to find anything wrong with a person, but things are obvious to children because their minds are constantly working.

In order to get to the bottom of a lot of the issues that we have in our families, we have to establish trust, boundaries, and rules of engagement within the family. We must be willing to talk about the tough subjects that arise, and we must not run from them, but face them head on. Gone are the days of passing down generational curses - today is the day we start passing on generational blessings.

Man is what he believes.

- Anton Chekhov

Chapter 2

The Grasshopper

Joseph is in a relationship with Tiana, and he doesn't know how to express how he really feels about her, so he always wants to show her through sexual intercourse. Tiana is in a situation where she doesn't know how to handle it, so she thinks that he is a sex addict and eventually decides to break up with him. A few weeks pass, and Joseph is with another woman and seems happy, but to Tiana he has rushed into another relationship. Joseph doesn't see anything wrong with being with another woman that fast because he doesn't want to be alone.

What Joseph hasn't told Tiana is that he has never had anyone to tell him that they love him, so he doesn't know how to express that to anyone. So he thinks that in order to show love, you have to have sex instead of talking about things of importance. Many men go through this, because they are raised in homes where the parents work a lot or they don't show emotion in the home. Also, generational curses play a major role in men becoming this way. A generational curse is basically a cycle that repeats itself in a family, but it has to be broken at some point, and why not with you? A lot of times when we think about demons, we think about a mystical being that is going to try to work its way inside of us, but that's not true at all. Demons are assigned to your family and they are what keep the generational curses going from one person to the next.

Generational curses are so severe that they can be passed on from your parents and grandparents. It is difficult for someone to be something they've never seen before, and generational curses are reasons why men go through their joy-fall experience. Men need to be taught how to approach situations, because it doesn't come naturally to a man to know that it's wrong to be with more than one woman at a time. The funny thing is, if you look back at stories that were written in the Bible, like the story of Adam and Eve, you see that Adam was so stunned when he woke up and saw Eve he could do nothing but say "WO-MAN!!!" Men are so stunned by the beauty and the figure of a woman that they can do nothing but think about her beauty, and it causes them to forget about themselves sometimes.

Young guys have to be taught how to look at a woman, how to talk to a woman, and how to handle a woman. A harsh reality is that young men are not often taught to save themselves for marriage, so they try to do too much too quickly, and sometimes it's with the wrong woman. The funniest thing to me is that everyone tells their daughters "baby, save yourself for marriage, and don't give no man your prized possession", but no one is telling the young men in the world that same thing. NEWS FLASH! These young men are doing stuff with those same young ladies who are being told these things at home, but the difference is the message never gets relayed to the males. Young men need to be taught the same thing, because there are so many television shows out now that make it seem like having a baby as a teen is cool, and it seems like it is being glorified.

Parents need to take an active approach, because it is best to allow your children to hear the truth about sex from their parents instead of from another child or the television. I believe that if young women and young men were taught the same principles, maybe the results we see in their future wouldn't be as bad as they are now. The devil watches how parents raise their children, just like everyone else does, and he knows just what tools to use on your son that will keep him in an internal battle for the rest of his life. What is typically going on in a situation like this is that the man has a void in his heart that needs to be filled and his mental state isn't stable.

Many men try to follow their heart, but mentally, they are fighting against what their heart is saying. Even the Bible talks about this in Galatians 5:17 "for the flesh desires what is contrary to the Spirit, and the Spirit what is contrary to the flesh. They are in conflict with each other, so that you are not to do whatever you want. So we all must remain aware of this so we understand the importance of praying for our spirit to become stronger than our flesh." The spirit you have was in existence before you had a body, so learn to let that lead instead of your flesh. Often, people say "He's thinking with the wrong head!" and often this is true. As men get older, often there are many mistakes made before we figure out life and what we shouldn't be doing anymore. I encourage you all now to truly find out who you are and the things that you need to rid yourself of before you pursue a relationship with someone that may not be for you anyway. We end up with the wrong people when we are the wrong person in that season.

It's funny how we have to think to think, right? Yeah, I said it right, you have to think to think! What I mean is this: in order for me to truly find out who I am and what I have to offer someone, I have to learn to think beyond the surface of who I am. A lot of times, men will identify themselves by what they do and not who they are. So what happens is that the young lady that you take out on a date will know more about what you do instead of who you are. Then she'll fall in love with what you do instead of who you are, and you'll be left wondering why she doesn't know you or anything about you, but she seems to be in love with your career choice. The thing about it is that you will start to hear her tell her friends about everything you do and nothing about who you are, but don't allow yourself to get upset with her, because you created that monster because you were confused. We have to be in tune with ourselves and our creator so that we know the difference between who we are and what we do, and so that we will know what we have to offer.

If you keep on saying things are going to be bad, you have a good chance of being a prophet.

Isaac Bashevis Singer

Chapter 3

Playing with Fire

John and Tiffany are in a relationship and they have a 2-year-old son named John Jr. Tiffany seems to be losing interest in John and he notices it. He begins to question himself about what could possibly be wrong with him. One day, they get into an argument about an ongoing issue with her being on her cell phone all the time, and she tells John "I can talk to whoever I want to, you're not my daddy." John says "Tiffany, who is he? I know it has to be a man on the phone!" She throws the phone and charges towards John. She scratches his face and neck so badly that he has blood pouring down from his face and neck all over his shirt and instead of fighting back, he just leaves the house. She taunts him by calling his cell phone time and time again.

Finally, she leaves a message on his phone stating, "You are a weak man, you are nothing to me!! You are just a tired, sorry punk that don't know how to handle his business or a woman!! I don't need you, and oh, let me tell you, Little J ain't even yours! Ha, ha, ha, now run and tell THAT! When I'm on the phone, I'm talking to his real daddy, which is something you'll never be!" John checks his messages and hears every word, and the situation hurts John down to the core. John doesn't know what to do when he initially hears the message, so he sits in his car for three hours and just cries. After the third hour, he becomes enraged and wants to go to the house to kill Tiffany. He starts the car, and a song is playing on the radio entitled *We Fall Down But We Get Up*, and instantly John changes his route of travel. He goes to the nearby church, falls on his knees, and screams "Lord help me, I don't know what to do! PLEASE HELP ME!!" He prays that God will help him in his time of need, because he doesn't know what else to do.

After four weeks go by, John finally builds up enough courage to call Tiffany to ask for a DNA test. Tiffany tells him "You ain't taking my baby nowhere to get no test done." John says 'okay', and hangs up the phone so he can come up with a plan to get the test done. A month goes by, and he finally gets the opportunity to pick up the child from daycare to get the test done at a nearby clinic. After he got the test done, he dropped John Jr. off to his mom and went home. John waited for about two weeks for the results and the anxiety started to set in. After the two weeks went by, he got the results in the mail and he found out that Little J was indeed his son. John fell to his knees and broke down crying.

This scenario is a reality for a lot of men in the world. In today's world, a lot of men see and hear of this kind of stuff happening, and there's not too much that can be done without a DNA test. A lot of men walk away from their child/children in situations like this, because they can't deal with the hurt, pain, and suffering that has been issued to them. Also, men all over the world are given a bad name because of those who choose to not take care of their children.

It's sad, because a lot of times, the men that really want to be there for their children never had a father of their own, and they know how it feels to not have one, so they want to do everything they can to be there for their child.

Many times in life, how a father and mother break up determines what happens with their child. I would like to encourage all men who are in this situation, who have been in this situation, and those who may eventually go through it to never give up fighting for your child. You just need to get access to a lawyer and go to court to ensure that no one can take your rights away from you. Also, if you are in a waiting period to see your child because the mother doesn't want you to see them, send a check every month to help support your child, because paying nothing only hurts the child.

Don't worry about what the mom might be doing with the money, because if the child isn't being taken care of and you're sending money, it will be a known thing. Allow yourself to be the bigger person and take care of your responsibility. Also, if you are in a situation of not knowing if a child is yours, continue to support the child until you find out, and if you are a man of God and you are the only father in the child's life, it may be a wise decision to never stop supporting the child. I know you're probably saying "this guy is crazy!" Think about it like this: if it were you in the child's place, what would you want? Would you want the only father you'd ever known to walk away from you with no explanation? There are men in the world who provide and sacrifice for their children, which brings me to the next scenario.

What one believes to be true either is true or becomes true within limits to be found experientially and experimentally. These limits are beliefs to be transcended.

- John Lilly

Chapter 4

The Work Horse

Jacob is a father of two (son and daughter) and he is doing everything he can for his children. He works as a computer systems technician, and he works 40 hours or more every week. He spends quality time with his children and ensures he doesn't miss any important events, which include PTA meetings, school graduations and awards ceremonies, basketball games, football games, cheerleading meets, track meets, ballet lessons, and softball games. Jacob is trying to catch up on a few bills that weren't paid during his divorce process and is need of assistance. He goes down to the public assistance office, and he is looked upon like he is less than a man when they find out that he's a single father and he has no savings in his account.

He was told he made $15.00 too much money, and therefore could not receive assistance from the government. Jacob wanted to take on another job, but knew he wouldn't be able to spend time with his children like he should, so he settled for one job and continued to live pay check to pay check. Many questions went through his head about why men can't get the same assistance as women, and why all men are looked as if they aren't there for their children. The reality is that there are a lot of single fathers in the world, and their sacrifices go unnoticed by the public. Ask yourself the question, "Are single fathers less significant than single mothers?"

In my opinion, I don't think so, because I was a single father and dealt with the same issue as Jacob. Many people looked at me like I was a foreign creature when they found out I was doing everything on my own, and I also had a sibling living with me as well. My goal was not to go out and beg anyone for anything, but it was to ensure that my son and I had everything we needed. Times did get hard, but I never regretted my son or the decisions I made to be a great father to him. The reality of my story is that I was a part of the US Air Force, and my son and I moved from an overseas location. I was told that we could get WIC when we came to the states, so I went down to the office and was told I made too much money.

They looked over all my bills and my income and said "Mr. Kinney, you make 15.00 too much, so you can't be approved." I thought to myself "what if I hadn't come down to the office and really was in need?" What if that $15.00 was all we had after I paid my mortgage, gas bill, light bill, water and trash bill, day care and food? Would they care more then? Would they care more if I was a family member of theirs or they knew me personally?" All of these questions went through my head, but I never gave up hope. Even though times were hard for me, I kept the faith and I moved forward.

I realized through that experience at the WIC office how blessed I really was, because I said to myself, "at least I have a mortgage to pay." Most people at the age of 22 don't have a mortgage because they aren't focused on that type of stuff yet. I realized how much more mature I was than the average 22-year-old through this experience as well, because most of my peers at the time were focused on getting new cars and clothes. I would often ask people, "Why do people complain so much about money when they make the same amount of money I make, and I have child and they don't?"

The answer to that question is quite simple: because people that don't have kids try to justify why they deserve everything, so they buy stuff, but when you're a parent, you realize you have to make responsible decisions, because it doesn't only affect you, but the child is affected as well. Many people look at the negative things in their life and don't try seeing the positive at all until some unforeseen circumstance causes them to reevaluate their life. I would like to encourage you to look at things in a positive light and watch how things start turning around for the better.

Always remember that the answers that you seek so often lie within you and not around you. You must look inside yourself and see what your creator sees in you, and the funny thing is, the creator knows because the things inside you were placed inside you at birth. All of your desires, dreams, and passions were already there, and now it is time that you tap into that so that you can start to reach your full potential and live life with no regrets. It is time out for excuses, because you owe yourself too much, and you owe the next generation too much to just let time slip by and never leave a footprint here on earth.

Your footprint is important, because it shows the next generation where to pick up the torch. The torch is meant to be carried on, just like you see when it's time for the Olympics to begin. Also, always remember this: don't try to take fast steps, because you will only leave a toe print, which can be confused for an animal, but dig your heels in so that your foot print is obvious and it won't be mistaken for something that it's not.

People only see what they are prepared to see.

- Ralph Waldo Emerson

Chapter 5

Who Am I?

The scenario discussed in the last chapter is also becoming the norm in America because the courts aren't always ruling in the women's favor anymore. More men are running the household without mothers being there, but they aren't valued as much as single mothers. When a man is treated like he is less than a man should be, he doesn't see the use in trying anymore, which isn't just true for many men but also for many little boys. It is time that the world realizes that the little boys that are soon to be men have feelings and emotions just like everybody else.

We as a human race need to realize how important it is to express how we feel without feeling like we are going to be embarrassed or condemned for what we say or do. It is important that we all feel like we can go to someone and really get the help we need, without a lot of strings attached. For men specifically, it's important to talk about what is bothering you, because no one can read your mind and everyone looks at life differently. Many men go through identity issues because of the lack of a father figure and positive male role models in the home or in the community where they live.

I remember growing up and seeing the guys who lacked attention at home. A lot of those guys ended up acting out in school for attention and getting suspended. A lot of them began to hang with the wrong crowds and ended up in jail because they felt like they needed to prove themselves to the guys in the streets. A lot of them started getting involved with drugs and drinking because they felt like no one cared about them. Personally, I felt like I didn't have much of a father figure at home. My father died when I was very young, and I didn't know what death was until he never came back. One day, my mom told me she was getting married and we were moving to another area. After my mom was married and moved, we began our new life.

I remember asking my stepfather to spend time with me by playing football and doing the stuff I was actually interested in doing, and I was always told "I'm tired!" As a child, always hearing that messed me up, because I thought I wasn't worth his time or effort. One day, I decided, "I'm going to start just playing by myself", and I believe God birthed something in me at that time. I began to play music more and more every day, and I started seeking out the things I was interested in, like football and baseball. I remember taking an old mattress and cutting a hole in it, just so I could practice pitching the ball.

Even though I never became a professional baseball player, I learned a lot about myself. I found out I was a very unique thinker, and I also learned that if I just focused my mind on something, I could accomplish the goal. I learned how independent I was through the circumstance of not having anyone to help me, and I also learned to listen to that still-small voice in my head that told me to never give up.

A lot of people go through life saying they don't know what they are supposed to be doing, but in all actuality, you may have heard it or even seen it before. It is very important that we listen to the things that God places before us, and I was always told if more than three people tell you the same thing, such as "You are really good at that, you should keep that up", this is something you may want to listen to. Personally, throughout my life I have heard "God has placed something inside of you, you have to stop running from it." I can honestly tell you I ran like Forrest Gump when I was told what I would be doing.

Now I'm an ordained minister preaching the gospel and never thought this would be my life. In life we have things that we want to do, but what matters is that we fulfill our purpose ,which is why we all are here on earth. Some say "I want to be happy and live a good life", you will do that when you do the things that you are meant to do instead of forcing yourself into something that doesn't fit you and/or you don't fit it. I'll give you a perfect example: I tried to do secular comedy after I realized secular comedians got more laughs than me in the clubs, so I wanted to figure out why. After watching a few comedians on stage, it didn't take long for me to figure out what was different about me. They cursed on stage and talked about all kinds of things like sex, drugs, violence, and other things that didn't have meaning to me because I didn't live like that. I knew my life consisted of things like the military and wanting to have better things in my life, like good credit, a family, God, etc.

Instead of me being comfortable with just being me, I stooped to a very low level, and on that night I decided to try what they were doing and see what happened. After my performance was over, I realized people laughed so much more than they had before, so I embarked on a new journey. I knew it wasn't right for me, but I tried to keep things going the way they were going because I noticed money started pouring in.

After a few months of this new life and new act on stage, I realized that I felt empty on the inside and needed something better in my life, but I kept worrying. "How do I tell people that this isn't really my act? How do I change what I have been doing for the past few months that have seemed to work so well for me? How do I keep the bookings and the money coming if I switch my act?" These are the questions that raced through my head, but I knew I had to make a serious decision that would alter my plans.

After I decided to stop putting on this show for people and do things the right way by not cursing and having real substance for people to learn from, I felt better. Even though the bookings slowed down and the money stopped pouring in, I was happy knowing that what I was bringing to the table was really me and not just an act. I also realized that it's not all about money, because people need to feel like they have learned something when they come to see a performer do what he or she does.

One of the main things I realized in this situation was that I lost sight of my goal and I didn't take into consideration how many people I could have possibly blessed with just being me and not putting on a show/act. My goal since I was a child was to be a professional musician/saxophonist and actor. I never wanted to be a comedian, but I was told when I was very young how funny I was and that maybe I should try comedy. After I started doing comedy, I realized that a lot of comedians used comedy as a platform to get movie roles and some of them became activists for major movements in the country. When I chose to change my performance, I made comedy a number one priority in my life and it took over me for a while.

I was taking on personalities of people that I was around a lot, and that was very dangerous for me and it didn't feel normal at all. After giving my life back to God, I realized that I had gone through one of the craziest experiences ever because I chose to be greedy. I wasn't happy with what I had and wanted what other people were getting, which was more laughs. I pray that you who read this book learn from my experience and never allow yourself to become greedy like I did.

To think of losing is to lose already.

- Sylvia Townsend Warner

Chapter 6

What are My Options?

Jordan is a high school student who is being raised by his grandmother. Jordan doesn't wear what he thinks are the best clothes or the best shoes to school, and he is intimidated by the other students. One day, he was on break for lunch, and a few students walked up to him and said, "Hey boy, why you always so dirty?" Jordan replied, "I'm not dirty, why do you all keep messing with me? I haven't done anything to anybody, but you guys always start to mess with me every day!"

One of the students put his finger in Jordan's face and they begin to fight. One of the teachers rushed in and broke them up and asked, "What is wrong with you all? Why are you all fighting?" Jordan replied, "They came over here to mess with me and they called me dirty." The teacher said, "All of you, let's go right now. We are going to the office!" When they walked into the office, the principal didn't ask any questions, but immediately told them they were all suspended from school for five days for fighting.

While Jordan was out of school on suspension, he sat at home on the porch, and on the second day there was a knock at the front door. Jordan answered and replied, "What's up, man? Who are you looking for?" The unfamiliar guy replied, "I'm looking for Jordan, are you Jordan?" Jordan says, "I'm Jordan, what's up?" The guy said, "I heard what happened to you, man, and I wanted you to know, we took care of that for you. Come walk with me real quick." Jordan was thinking to himself, "How did this guy hear about what happened to me?"

Even though Jordan was nervous about leaving the house with a total stranger, he wanted to know more about the guy, so they left the house and went to another house where a lot of guys were standing around playing cards. A tall guy, about 6'6", stood up and said, "What up, lil' Jordan, come let me holla at you." Jordan walked with him, and he asked Jordan to join his gang because they wanted to protect him and help him make some money. At first, Jordan was terrified, but after a few minutes of thinking about it, he figured "Why not!? They'll look out for me, and the kids at school won't mess with me anymore."

Jordan was initiated that evening and was now officially a part of the gang. So often, young men go through things like this, but it doesn't have to happen if we as a community could come together and look out for those who might be in need of assistance and love. Many young men in the world today don't require much, but what they do require is guidance and someone to listen to them when they need to talk or even vent. There were many times in my life where I remember being in the same situation, because my father died when I was six years old. I just wanted someone to hear what I needed to say about the things that really bothered me and some of the dreams I had.

When a young man feels like he doesn't fit in, he will do whatever it takes to feel accepted. One of the major problems with young men is that they need to feel validated, and they will do whatever it takes to get that validation. Another important aspect of the situation depicted is that a lot of men that make it to adulthood feel the need to buy a lot of materialistic stuff to feel like they are worth something to everyone around them. They don't realize that it is not the things that you buy that make you worth something, but the decisions that you make while stepping into manhood.

Those who I call the 'people pleasers' are never satisfied with the things they have, so they are always going out in search of more. Many of the people living in America right now are the same way, so you have a bunch of people who are chasing the same thing, which equates to nothing, and the sad thing is that they compare themselves to each other, which make everything worse. Even though this portion of the book is called "When His Joy Falls", that doesn't mean this is just a man's issue. People are living paycheck to paycheck right now because of something that has happened to them in their past, and they are trying to fill a void in their heart.

We all have to learn that the past doesn't have to play a major factor in our current situation or in our future. We have to learn to forgive those who have hurt us and let go of the things that have caused us disappointment. We all go through things that can and will cause us to react a certain way, but if we look at the things that we have been through as a blessing instead of a curse, we can began to be a blessing to other people, just as we are to ourselves.

Realize that your story is yours for a reason, and you have to tell someone about it, because they may have gone through the same things and may be able to help you start your healing process. Personally, in the beginning I didn't want to open up for the world to see my imperfections, but this is needed because so many people feel like they are all alone. But guess what? You're not! Though it may seem like many people are living the good life, you never know what's going on or what has gone on behind the scenes.

All men must understand that there is greatness within you, and no one can take that away from you. Yes, things may be rough at times, but we have so much greatness inside of us that we can overcome any and all things that may try to beset us. Know that in life you do indeed have options, and you dictate which options you are going to choose. No one can make that decision for you, and we have to stop allowing other people to have so much power over us that we allow them to make decisions for us.

When a person feels like they don't have options, they either want to give up or go straight into survival mode, and no one wants to feel that way. One of my favorite speakers is Earl Nightingale, and he says, "We are all self-made, but only the successful will admit it." Think about it, you'll never see a broke person say they are self-made! They are going to find somebody to blame for their problems, and they'll continue to blame more people if they never end up where they think they should be in life.

You probably know people like this too, and maybe you are one of the people you are thinking about. What I know is that if you stand around and never move, you can't blame anyone, because you have the power to move your body and if you don't, you can't blame those that are moving. It's funny how people will say things like, "Look at them over there, thinking they are successful!" Really, the successful people don't ever think they are successful, because they are in constant pursuit of success and that's what drives them. What drives you? Do you know? You have to look deep within yourself.

What did you want to be when you were a child? Are you there or did you allow your hurt and pain to stop you? What are you afraid of? My other favorite speaker, Les Brown, says, "Everything is worth doing badly, but at least you tried."

You have reached the end of When His Joy Falls, now let's move on to the solutions entitled Upholding Standards!   These are sure to bless your life.

Upholding Standards

Being a man is not an easy task by any means.

The man that doesn't take a stand will fall.

Self-image sets the boundaries of
individual accomplishment.

- Maxwell Maltz

Chapter 7

Fear of Failure
Grabbing Fear By the Horns

The fear of failure is something that most men deal with on a daily basis until they grasp the concept of facing the thing that they fear the most. Being a man of God, I believe that fear is the devil's way of trying to control your potential, success, and destiny. We must all acknowledge that the devil's job is to rob us of the things that God has promised us all. We are very guilty of allowing our joy to be stolen based on one or two disappointments – because we don't know when to stop beating ourselves up over a "mess up". It is very important to pick ourselves up, dust ourselves off, and continue on, but we must learn from our mistakes. We are called to forgive as Christ has forgiven us, and the hardest thing is for a man to forgive himself, but we can do it. This has to become a learned behavior for men especially. We aren't taught how to forgive ourselves; we are taught how to be hard on ourselves when we do something wrong, and we're taught that it's not okay to cry, so we bottle up our feelings.

A perfect example is if you are playing sports and you miss either a pass in football or a jump shot in basketball, fathers and fans are quick to talk about what you didn't do right, but they never talk about the successes like they talk about the negatives. I was always told as a child that bad news travels faster than good news, which is true, and what I know is that negative news is brought up ten times more often than positive news is. For instance, if a young man graduates from high school and then graduates from college, the conversation about that will last maybe one or two days, but if the same young man chooses a different path and goes to jail, that conversation will last for several days or maybe even a couple of months. The primary reason we are afraid of failure is because we don't want to be the talk of the town and we don't need more pressure put on us than the pressure we already have, which is precisely what failure would bring. As stated earlier, it's the enemy's job to keep us from achieving the things that God wants us to have, and this can happen in a number of different ways, which I will elaborate on.

Many men have experienced things in their past that cause them to believe certain things. For instance, if a young man doesn't have a strong male figure at home, or anywhere in his life for that matter, he will face issues with guidance and direction. Among the questions that ring in his head is, "What do I want to do? I've never talked about it with anyone." Many men deal with identity issues so they think to themselves, "Who am I? What do I want to be when I get older?" All of these questions remain unanswered until a man builds up enough nerve to ask someone for help, or he just ends up in the right place at the right time and someone is there to give him advice about life.

It is very important for a young man to have someone in his life to help guide him and take an interest in the things that could shape him into the man he is really supposed to be. The goal of a man should be to reach his full potential before he leaves this world, but how can a man do that if he doesn't have help and guidance? Primarily, the world puts emphasis on the parents being at home when it comes to raising children, but it takes an entire village to raise a child. That's one of the things that we are missing in today's world.

Most children today witness more fights between adults now than they did when I was growing up. Back in the day, I often saw two parents talk about an issue and they worked it out without getting mad and upset, but today's parents fight first and ask questions later. This is not something you want a young man to see, especially when he is being raised in a home that is lacking love, support, encouragement, and guidance. In order to raise a boy into a man, there must be many positive influences, including those that come from outside the home.

Men deal with numerous issues because of things they see on television and the internet. My greatest fear used to be ending up back in my home town and working in a factory. The reason

I feared that was because I was able to go and experience the world outside of my hometown, and I saw and heard stories of people going back home because they fell into hard times. I never wanted to move back home to live with my mother, because I knew women weren't in favor of that, and I knew people would talk negatively of me if I did that. Another one of my fears was going to war. Due to my being in the US Air Force, I was called to deploy.

I learned a lot about myself during the deployment, because I was forced to be isolated from the world as I knew it, and was placed in a situation where I had to face a lot of issues I would typically run from. Prior to leaving for my deployment, my brother passed away, and I tried to keep myself very busy so I would keep my mind off of the loss. I was in Kuwait a few months after his death and I had to learn how to let go of my brother. I had to learn not to torture myself with thoughts such as, "What he could have done with his life if he had lived?" and "If he would have had children, would they be close to my children like we were?" I also learned during that time how much I needed my saxophone in my life. I played every day and didn't realize how much God was dealing with me until I played and burst into tears.

So, the very thing I feared was actually a true blessing to me. Now I play my saxophone all over the world and the music I'm blessed to be able to play is helping people all over the world in different ways. Now, I don't know what you have gained from this chapter, but I hope that you gained a better understanding of the reality of fear and how you have to grab it by the horns and control it. Don't let fear drive you away from your destiny.

Remember that time waits on no one, and you don't have time to waste. My piece of commentary is that your days are numbered, and a man born of a woman has just a few days and they are full of trouble. You might ask "what trouble?" and the trouble is the thoughts and actions that we have when trying to figure out this thing called life. Every moment you spend on earth must be treasured and taken seriously, because you never know when your last moment will be, so seize every moment. Try to see the blessings in everything instead of looking for the negative, because in everything there is a lesson to be learned. I would rather try something and do it horribly than to not try it at all and hope and wish. Should haves, could haves, and would haves are always at the tips of the tongues of those that didn't try something that they had the power in their mind to do, but they didn't allow their thoughts to sync up with their body.

Immense power is acquired by assuring yourself in your secret reveries that you were born to control affairs.

- Andrew Carnegie

Chapter 8

Validation
Am I good enough?

When a man has been placed in a situation that has caused him to grow up fast or without the presence of a father figure, many issues reside within him. Many men deal with the issue of validation – a need to feel validated and accepted by others. For those that don't thoroughly understand what validation is, it is simply when you feel like you need people to say or do something for you to prove your worth. I have personally dealt with this issue because I didn't feel confident in my worth and couldn't tell anyone the truth about it. People would ask me questions about who I was, and I would always define myself by my job, my talents, and anything else I felt had value or carried weight. I remember having conversations with people and they would say, "so, tell me a little about yourself." My mind would start racing really quickly, because I wanted to tell the person about all of my television appearances, all of the awards I had received in the military, and all of the money I had made and all of the places I'd been. After about two years of this, I realized I really wasn't telling anyone about myself, and this was the reason why people never really could get to know me.

When you define yourself by the things that you have done, you are setting yourself up for failure. Many people love to hear stories about the things you have done and all the places you have been just so they can use you and abuse you. The greatest thing you can do is tell people about who you really are. For example, you may say, "I'm a man of God, I love being around people, I'm very outgoing, I love children, I love having fun, I love music, I love to write." These are the things that people need to know about you, because they can really see if a friendship is even possible with you. Many times I have found myself in situations when people thought all I could do was talk about my comedy and music career. I remember another time in my life when people thought all I could do was curse a lot and drink a lot of beer. That isn't the image I wanted to portray to people. I didn't want to suck up my pride and ask for guidance from anyone. I thought to myself, "I can figure this out on my own; nobody is going to help me anyway."

I allowed myself to think this way for quite a while, until one day I went to church in Kaiserslautern, Germany. I heard a preacher talking about how men feel the need to be validated. He mentioned that instead of looking to the world for validation, people should go to God. I thought to myself, "Oh snap, this is just what I need to hear right now!" Then, the preacher said, "God cares enough about you to show you your identity and all you have to do is ask him and he'll show you." I thought to myself, "Well, I should probably jump up and ask him right now!" However, I realized that wasn't the appropriate thing to do, so I stayed seated and after the service, I walked up to talk to the preacher. He told me he would pray with me and he would help me to find my way.

After a few weeks passed by I found myself thinking differently, because we would pray and just ask God to show me my identity because I was lost, and he revealed it more and more every day. God also showed me that I was looking in all the wrong places, looking to the wrong people and doing the wrong things trying to find my identity. So for those of you who may not know who you are, what you are supposed to do, or where you are supposed to go in your life, simply ask the one who created you, and you'll be surprised when you get your answer. Don't rush him to answer you; just wait and be patient, and your answer will come.

Also, the truth of the matter is that your family will try to tell you who they think you should become, and that seems okay, but the reality is that as you grow older, your family has to get to know you just like you have to get to know you. Things change with every person every day, because there are some things that you learned yesterday that you are either applying today or trying to figure out the meaning today. Life doesn't deal everyone the same hand, so you can't listen to an individual that is confused about life and expect for them to give you sound guidance.

A lot of times, the people that we seek validation from are looking for validation themselves. Think about it! How many times have you gone to ask for advice from an individual and they've turned around and asked you for some form of advice? What about a time where you've gone to ask someone what they think about your clothing or your car and they ask you the same question? A lot of times, we associate with the same type of people that we are on the inside and because the internal thing that draws us together isn't easily seen, we don't know why we hang around certain types of people.

Validation isn't always a bad thing, but it can be bad if it comes from the wrong place and the wrong people. Validation can be used as a manipulation tool to keep you feeling stuck or obligated to do something for someone, so we have to be careful who we seek validation from. Most times we think that it's just a female issue, but that is very far from the truth. Validation is a gender neutral issue that we all must learn to check, just like our attitude and our motives.

One of the things we all must understand, starting now, is that we actually put pressure on ourselves and the people that we seek the validation from. When you look for someone to show you who you are and expect for them to give you the pat on the back that you feel like you need, you're giving too much power to that person. It's just like being in a relationship and expecting your partner to make you happy. You have to be happy with yourself and that is the bottom line. The funny thing about the situation with validation is that we look to those who want to feel validated too.

Also, just to make it even more direct for you, we try to impress those that try to impress us, and we end up competing for attention, time, space and validation. It's like two blind people trying to lead each other in an area that they have no knowledge of. This will never turn out to be a pretty situation, so we must focus our energy on the things that matter in life.

The greatest discovery of my generation is that man can alter his life simply by altering his attitude of mind.

- William James

Chapter 9

Making the Right Choices
Which way do I turn?

All men deal with having to make difficult decisions that can either make or break them. A lot of men lose it when it is time to make difficult decisions, especially when they are trying to provide for their family. Many men are dealing with being laid off and having to find employment, and some may feel as if they don't make enough money to support their family. In today's world, many families are being torn apart due to the struggling economy, but your family doesn't have to be. Decisions have to be made fast in our world, because you never know what tomorrow may bring. It is important to stay focused and believe that God can, and will, bring you through tough situations. I honestly remember thinking about leaving the military and collecting my disability, but I was afraid because I knew my family wouldn't have medical insurance if I did that.

The reality of the situation is that if I am a true believer in Christ, I shouldn't be worried about the stuff that doesn't matter. I'm not saying that medical insurance doesn't matter, but worrying about stuff like that is unnecessary because if God has provided a job, as well as medical insurance, for me for this long, why would I need to worry about that now? Let me share a secret with you: "When you worry, you tell God that you don't trust him." Also, when you worry, you tend to want to do something about the thing you are worrying about, while God may be saying to you, "Be patient and wait on me to work some things out on your behalf." When you try to jump in there and make things happen, you are guaranteed to mess it up. Look at it like this: you are traveling down the highway and there's construction on the road. You see that the crew is working on the road and they know what they are doing, but because you get slowed down in traffic you get upset and worried about making it to your destination on time. You jump out of the car and you tell the crew to move and let you through. Now, what you don't know is that the road isn't a flat surface and it has a sink hole in it so there's a detour, but because you are so upset, you don't allow the crew to tell you about the detour. So they move like you asked them to and you spin your tires and drive on through as fast as you can and you end up in the sink hole. Because of the heat of the moment, you are not on the detour route but in the path of danger and you don't know it. That is exactly how it is with life sometimes, because instead of us waiting on guidance to make a decision, we become impatient and we make decisions that can cause damage.

Making hasty decisions isn't necessary, because the guidance is there if we just allow the directions to be given to us through prayer.

Prayer is a mandatory thing for us all, because in order to know what we have to do, we have to ask the right questions, and sometimes we don't get answers in the timing that we want. Just to help you out with this, here is a simple prayer you can use to get started. "Dear Heavenly Father, in the name of Jesus, I thank you for allowing me the opportunity to pray right now and acknowledging the fact that I need you. I thank you for my life, health, and strength. I also thank you for being a guide in my life and I ask that you show me what I am supposed to be doing with this life that you gave me. Without your help, I will be lost. Lord, with you I can accomplish great things, but without you I can accomplish nothing. I need you to teach me how to become more like you and trust you with my very being, and I need you every day of my life. Let your will be done in my life, God. I pray this prayer right now, in the name of Jesus Christ of Nazareth, Amen."

If you start with a prayer like this, you are on your way to a new beginning. It is important that we as men learn that we can't do anything on our own that will turn out right, because we have to go back to the source of our strength, which is God.

Each of us makes his own weather, determines the color of the skies in the emotional universe which he inhabits.

- Fulton J. Sheen

Chapter 10

Dealing with Loss

A lot of men deal with pride issues that won't allow them to ask for help.

I have personally had to deal with this issue a few times in my life, and I didn't realize how my pride was getting the best of me until someone pointed it out. Many people don't realize how fast your pride will sneak up on you and get the best of you, and you'll start to think that you are crazy, but you're really not. I lost my dad at a very young age, and I didn't know who to talk to about it or if anyone would understand what I was going through.

I began to act out instead of trying to seek help. After the initial start of the acting out, I started to realize how I felt when I would get disciplined for it. My mom would always ask me, "Boy, what is wrong with you?" and I wouldn't know what to tell her, so I continued to act out and fight all the time in school. A few months went by, and my mom came to the school and jacked me up in front of my teachers and the principal. They all asked me the same question: "Demoine, why are you doing this? What is really going on with you?" After sitting there in a chair feeling isolated, I simply told them, "I miss my daddy and I don't know why I feel the way I do all the time." The teachers and my mom looked at each other and I heard one of them say, "He is grieving the loss of his father, but doesn't know how to express that because he doesn't naturally know how to deal with loss."

Just like me, a lot of people go through this same situation or something similar at a very young age, and the outcome is sometimes the same. For others, the outcome can be a life long ordeal, because some people think, "no one will ever understand me, because they aren't me." I'm here to tell you that loss is something we all have to deal with at some point in life. It doesn't matter if it's a parent, sibling, grandparent, friend, cat, dog, fish, or whatever – loss is a thing that we all must learn to deal with the right way.

People can feel like they are backed into a corner, which causes them to feel like they have to fight their way out. Truthfully, this is a natural feeling for anyone, so for those that feel like they are fighting for what they want or fighting for what they need, this isn't an unnatural feeling. No one wants to be backed into a corner and no one wants to feel isolated, so the best thing that you can do is learn to talk about your issues and ordeals with those that you really love and those who really love you.

A lot of people look only at the loss of people, but I'm here to tell you that loss of life isn't the only type of loss that we all experience. We can experience loss of jobs, homes, marriages, relationships with your children, and many other types of loss. We have to learn how to deal with these things, because carrying things along with you can be very dangerous. We need to learn how to let go.

I heard a saying a couple of years ago that makes a lot of sense, and it says, "Hurt people hurt people." There's nothing in the world like dealing with a person who has been hurt, because they carry that hurt with them and it makes life seem so unfair to that person. It also makes the person feel like they can't trust anyone and they seem to always be in a defensive stance. This isn't just true for men, but a lot of times it's harder for men to admit that they have been hurt. For instance, I remember being at an event and seeing a fight break out between two men.

The guy who was on the bottom was bleeding profusely, and when a few other people finally separated the fighters, the guy who had been beat up said, "Man, get off me. I'm good, he didn't hurt me!" I was looking at him thinking, "Man, yes he did; you must not be seeing the same thing we are seeing." His face was busted and his lips was as fat as a gremlin's lips, but he was trying to convince everybody that he wasn't hurt. Men, it is time that we stop trying to always be macho and tell the truth about how we feel. No one can help you if you don't say you need the help. Remember this: "Pride comes before the fall." If you allow pride to get the best of you, it will cause you to fall by the wayside and you will feel very isolated. With this comes the devil's mind games of making you feel like you are not worthy and that no one cares, but the right thing to do to prevent all of this is to express how you really feel on the inside to someone you trust.

"Do not base your success on what other people are doing, but what you want out of your life and what you are happy with. Success isn't something that can be measured based on other people, but you and your happiness."

Demoine Kinney

Chapter 11

Defining Success and Your Right To Be Great!

Many men define success by how much money they have, the kind of car they drive, the size house in which they live in, and the look of the woman they have on their arm. I can completely understand this way of thinking, but I can also tell you that it is wrong. The right way of thinking isn't based on materialistic belongings, but is based on happiness. Some may say, "What?!! THAT'S CRAZY!!" I can honestly tell you that I have had a lot of material things for a while now, including houses, cars, motorcycles, women, a dog, money, and everything else you could probably name; yet, I lacked happiness because I felt like nothing was ever enough. I used to look around to see what else I could get in my life but nothing seemed to work for me.

One particular day I was sitting at home looking around at everything that I had acquired, and I noticed that everything that I had was looking great, but I was all by myself and it didn't feel that good. I began to think about what it would be like to share my life with that special someone, and also I thought to myself, "What would it feel like to be closer to God?" I used to hear people all the time talk about how they were at peace when they began to live life with and for God. They seemed so happy, even when they went through tough times. I didn't quite understand that, because I was used to hearing people complain about what they didn't have.

I also noticed that people didn't have a solution in mind to fix their situation. After hearing all of the things I had heard and experiencing the things that I had experienced, I began to search for things in the Bible. On my first day of opening the Bible, I was amazed at how everything seemed to flow and apply to my situation. I started with New Testament scriptures and I moved forward from there. What really surprised me was the fact that I was raised in the church and had never heard any of the scriptures that I was reading.

I only remember people shouting around the church and saying the same stuff every week, like "Matthew 4:4 Man shall not live by bread alone but by every word that proceeded out of the mouth of God." I also heard stuff such as, "Psalms 150:6 let everything that has breath praise the Lord." I remember hearing things about going through trials and tribulations and how to seek God. I heard the scripture, "Matthew 6:33 Seek ye first the kingdom of God and his righteousness; and all these things shall be added unto you," but I never heard anyone explain how to do that. What I do know now at this point in my life is that I must become a servant to God and allow him to work on my behalf, and all the things that he has for me will be for my good. I said all of this because a lot of times we go in search of the wrong things in life but the right thing is to search for is God.

We tend to rely on other people to make us happy and tell us who we are, but the best place to start is with God. It doesn't matter whether you are a Christian right now or not, I challenge you to go to the one who made you the person that you are and ask, "Can you show me who I am in you?" Many of us allow other people to dictate the type of person that we are, but the funny thing is, the person dictating who you are may not even know who they are. It's just like the Bible says, "The blind leading the blind." I would rather go to God, who knows me better than I know myself, and get the right answers about who I am and the person that I am supposed to become.

I challenge you to seek God and allow him to tell you who you are. If you feel like you have gotten away from God, the way to start your journey back is to acknowledge the fact that you need God and you can do nothing without him. Apologize to God for trying to take his place by playing God in your own life. This is called repentance, and the only way to get back to God is through repentance, inviting God into your heart, mind and spirit, prayer, and studying God's word. Do not try to work your way into heaven because it's impossible, but focus on praying, studying the word, and fasting (going without food), because these things are pleasing to God simply because you're teaching your flesh that it doesn't have control of you or your decisions but instead that your spirit is in control. If you focus on pleasing God, you'll notice that a lot of the issues that people have are minor, because God can fix anything.

Now this may come as a surprise to you, but YOU HAVE A RIGHT TO SUCCEED!! That is your God-given right, and you must know this now! This is an affirmation you should say everyday: "I have a right to succeed, I have a right to grow, I have a right to expect great things in my life, and I have a right to be great!!" You have probably never in your life said this to yourself, or much less anyone else, but today I challenge you to step up into your greatness so that you can step out in faith.

You have the right to succeed in all that you do and there's nothing standing in your way that you don't allow. Yes, I said what you thought I said, "nothing that you don't allow!" Many people in life allow things to stand in the way of them succeeding, but they don't realize it, so they choose to blame outside sources for their shortcomings. What is shocking is the fact that many people don't realize that when you are born, the access that you need to succeed is readily available to each person. The things that are within you at birth are the abundance that the Bible talks about on many occasions. Some of us have allowed ourselves to think that the abundance spoken of in the Bible means material possessions, but it doesn't, it means potential.

I heard a great thinker and speaker by the name of Napoleon Hill say it like this: "We are born with two envelopes, which are the riches you may enjoy if you take possession of your mind and direct it to ends of your own choice, and the other is the penalties you must pay if you neglect to take possession of your own mind and direct it." (Think and Grow Rich, Napoleon Hill)

The thing that makes or breaks us all is our mind set. If our mind is limited, then we will be limited, and if our mindset is open, then we will be open to anything. We have to approach life with an open mind, because we never know what may come our way. Preparation is necessary in life, but we must prepare our minds and ensure that we properly condition them.

I'm reminded of a time where my uncle Pete was teaching me and my cousin how to catch a baseball, and he would hit the ball and say keep your eye on the ball. Once the ball would come close to us, we would run to the ball and open our glove to get ready for the ball to roll right on in. There were times when our focus was off and we would run past the ball, and there were times when we would have the ball in our glove and drop the ball, but my uncle kept repeating 'focus on the ball and keep your eye on it even when it is in your glove'. Some of us don't allow ourselves to see what we have in life, because we are not taught to seize the moment.

Your right to succeed is not up to other people, but it's up to you. You have to change your mind set in a way that you are not easily distracted, or like my favorite book says, not easily beset. Your mind has to be elevated so highly that you don't blame anyone for anything, and you don't blame situations and circumstances for anything either. It's so easy to blame people for things when things don't look that great, but it's even easier to take the responsibility and move on from it. Take notes of all the lessons learned so you don't make the same mistakes twice and move on.

Many of us think that taking a mental note is good enough, but that's not true, simply because we have so much going on in our heads that we forget the real decision that caused the mistake to happen. You can't just remember the mistake, but instead need to remember the decision which caused the mistake or mishap. I say this all the time, we have to think to think, which simply means this: get past your external thoughts and into your subconscious. One thing I do is sit in a silent room in my home, which is usually my man cave, and I elevate my feet. Once I'm totally relaxed, I clear my mind of anything that is negative and allow my mind to wander. Once I'm in the area of my subconscious that holds the secrets to success, I let them flow and I stay there for about 10 to 15 minutes. I try to have focused thinking time every day because my priority list comes from there. Often, we are taught to pray by talking, but I say pray by listening, because it's funny how you will be shown things, people, and places to pray for and about.

I pray that this book blessed you in a very special way, and know that I love you with the love of Jesus Christ. My goal with this book was to shed light on a few situations that we all may have faced in the past, and not just talk about it but provide solutions to getting over the hurt and pain from these situations. Your life belongs to you, so take ownership of it and never stop your pursuit of happiness. Understand this, though: your Spirit, Mind, and Body must be in tune with your creator in order to get to that happy place in life, because if it's not, things will always be out of sync, and you will take the world's approach, which says Mind, Body, and Soul.

I hope this has been a blessing to you.

God bless you,

Demoine Kinney

Don't let someone else's opinion of

you become your reality.

-Les Brown

Encouragement for You

I would like to use these next few pages to empower, inspire, and motivate you into your greatness. You have something inside of you that you were born with called greatness! No matter what you've been told in the past or even today, I'm here to tell you that you have greatness within you and there's nothing you can do about it. What you have to do is learn how to tap into the greatness that is within you so that you can become the man that you were created to be.

You were born with free will, but because you couldn't take care of yourself, you learned to be at the mercy of someone else's will. It's funny how many people will allow themselves to stay in that same state of mind for most of their life, when that is absolutely not how we were created. We were created to be independent but dependent at the same time. Some may ask the question,

"what does that mean?", and I have the answer to that question, but before I tell you, let me tell you this: you cannot live life for others and they can't live life for you.

So, to answer the question, it's simply that in life you go through stages which should look like this: you are born and your mother and father are your care givers. Upon turning about the age of nine months to a year, you learn to walk. When you are around the age of two or three, you begin to form not only a personality, but also an opinion. Around the age of four to six, you begin your school career, where you learn the things that are important in life and the history of human existence. At that point, your mind is being shaped and molded without your family, but your family does decide what school you attend. Out of this information that I just provided in a brief illustration format, you should have learned that no matter what you learn in life, your mind is being shaped and molded, and your family still is there to decide things for you.

At what stage in life should your family no longer have an influence on your mind and decision making? There are many people that struggle with this question because they don't want to deal with the thought of making a decision on their own and it possibly turning out to be a bad one. The influence that our family has on our mind is valuable, but at some point, you have to be able to make sound decisions without their assistance. One of my favorite speakers, Earl Nightingale, said "Most people only use 5% of their potential." My goal is to assist you in increasing that by showing you examples of those people that you may either watch on television or read about in magazines that overcame small thinking and had to truly find out the power of their will.

Most times, we see people in life and we believe that their will is stronger or even better than ours, but the truth to the matter is this: your will is just as powerful as theirs, but you have to learn how to tap into yours just like they did. You have greatness within you! If no one has ever told you that, I'm here to let you know now that YOU HAVE GREATNESS WITHIN YOU!! Say that to yourself every day, because studies have shown that it takes 16 positive messages to overcome 1 negative message that you either hear from someone else or from a self-inflicted negative comment. Greatness is within you and the thing about that is that you were born with it.

One of my favorite scriptures says this: "Before the foundation of the world was laid you were already chosen." I have a secret to share with you though, and it is that you were chosen to be great! You were not born and placed here on Earth to just take up space and breathe in air. You were placed here to change your environment with your creative thoughts and the things that your creativity will bring, not to just you but to those around you.

Now don't underestimate what I just said, because guess what, you can make an impact so big that you can affect even those that may never meet you. Do you think Tom Ford knew that he would affect people all over the world with the creation of the automobile, or do you think he only wanted to affect those that he could see and knew personally? That question alone should cause you to think more deeply about yourself, because most times we only focus on wanting to cause change within our eye sight, but you were created to cause change that surpasses your eye sight. Also, never be afraid to ask for help, because Rome was not built overnight, and it surely wasn't built by one person. In order to get to your destiny, you need assistance and guidance. Many of us think we can do everything ourselves, but this is very far from the truth. We all need a mentor and we all need a coach. There is absolutely nothing wrong with someone helping you to accomplish a goal, but you must ensure that the person you are soliciting for help has the same goal as you. Having a common goal gives both parties the means to become successful.

About The Author

Demoine Kinney, is an awesome man of integrity and a firm believer in God. He is the Pastor of Faith Builder's Ministries of Christ in Bishopville, South Carolina. He is also a US Air Force Decorated Veteran who served in Operations Iraqi Freedom, Iraqi Enduring Freedom, and the Syrian Crisis operations. He has been noted in interviews, stating, "My goal is to be a blessing to as many people as possible before I leave this Earth". He was cast in the blockbuster hit movie "The Avengers" as a Shield Agent, and it is one of America's top selling movies of all time, grossing

$683.1 million the first weekend.

Demoine is primarily known for his standup comedy, acting, and his career as a self-taught saxophonist. He has a passion for bringing a positive message to all audiences, young and old, with his unique style of sharing his testimony through his saxophone and humor. He realized early in his career that there are some people who need to be reached through music. Although he's a hilarious Christian comedian and actor as well, his first love was music. Today he is known to be an amazing saxophonist, and receives request to perform all over the country.

After losing his father at the age of six, he was given the gift of music, and carries his sax everywhere he goes. He tried to separate his gifts at one point, but soon realized that they were not given to exchange one for another, but to be used together in ministry. This anointed man of God now utilizes all the gifts to minister to the world.

www.DemoineKinney.com

Lastly, Demoine Kinney is the 2016 Democratic Candidate for the South Carolina House of Representatives District 50 Seat. His goals are to bring jobs, commerce, educational opportunity, and tourism to the District 50 area which includes Lee County, Kershaw County, and Sumter County. He was quoted as saying, "I believe God sent my family and I here to Bishopville, SC, to be a blessing by assisting with adding value to the community and discover some of the hidden talent and gifted people in the Lee County area."

2016 SC House of Representatives Democratic Candidate

Representing Lee, Kershaw and Sumter Counties